FOCUS ON

Comprehension

3

Stories by significant children's authors	Traditional stories, myths, legends, fables from other cultures	Stories from other cultures	Plays	Concrete poetry	Classic poetry	Narrative poetry	Poems from other cultures	Choral and performance poetry	Recounts	Observational records/reports	Instructional texts	Explanations	Persuasive writing
			✓								✓		
✓									✓				
				✓	✓								
	✓	✓											
	✓		✓						✓				
✓									✓				
												✓	✓
										✓		✓	✓
					✓				✓				
	✓	✓							✓				
	✓	✓											
			✓				✓	✓					
											✓	✓	
	✓	✓											
							✓						
	✓									✓		✓	
										✓		✓	
✓		✓				✓	✓		✓				
					✓	✓			✓				
✓	✓								✓				
✓									✓				
✓									✓				

Contents

UNIT 1   The Water Cycle

Think ahead

What do you think the word 'cycle' means in the title?

Start here ▶ Riding on high,   Clouds in the sky
          All over again   Looking like paper
        Ready to rain   But made up of vapour,
        Into the skies   Drift over hills
      Then the mists rise   Where the air chills.
      By the sun's rays.   Vapour condenses,
        Of watery haze   Rainfall commences
      Allows the creation   (Or dew on the grass
        And evaporation   Like breath on a glass)
        Gradually heats it   This trickles to give us
        There the sun greets it   Streamlets and rivers
          It reaches the seas.   Till by degrees

**From *Scholastic Poetry Collections*
by Noel Petty**

Water vapour turns into small droplets of water. These make clouds.

Clouds drop rain on hills and mountains.

Water is warmed by the sun. It turns into water vapour.

Streams and rivers carry the water back to the sea.

Thinking back

Write sensible answers to these questions.

1 What does water in the sea turn into when it is heated by the sun?
2 What does water vapour become in the sky?
3 When the clouds pass over hills or mountains what do they drop?
4 What carries the water back to sea?

Thinking about it

1 In what way could the clouds in the sky 'look like paper'?
2 Write the meaning to these words
   a) chills   b) condenses   c) commences
3 What name is given to a small stream?
4 Find another word in the poem that means the same as:
   a) mist   b) slowly   c) welcomes
5 Find the name given to a small drop of water in the diagram.

Thinking it through

1 How does the presentation of the poem help you think of the process it describes?
2 How do you know which way to read the poem?
3 What do you think of the poem? Give your reasons.
4 How does the diagram help you understand the process, or cycle, more easily?
5 What is the purpose of the labels in the diagram?
6 Which of the two texts opposite is written in prose and which is written in verse?

UNIT 2   The Moon of Gomrath

Think ahead

Look at the picture. What could have happened?

Colin woke suddenly and discovered his sister's bed was empty.

Colin tiptoed downstairs and groped his way to the door. It was still bolted. Had Susan dropped nine feet to the cobbles? He eased the bolts, and stepped outside, and as he looked he saw a thin silhouette pass over the skyline of the Riddings.

Colin ran: and by the time he stood up at the top of Clinton Hill he had halved the lead that Susan had gained. For it was undoubtedly Susan. She was wearing her pyjamas. Straight ahead of her were the dark tops of the trees in the quarry.

'Sue!' No, wait. That's dangerous. She's sleep-walking. But she's heading for the quarry. Colin ran as hard as he had ever run. He came to the fence that stood on the edge of the highest cliff and looked around while he recovered his breath.

The moon showed all the hill-side and much of the quarry: the pump tower gleamed, and the vanes turned. But Susan was nowhere to be seen. Colin searched the sides of the quarry with his eyes, and looked at the smooth black mirror of the water. He was frightened. Where was she?

Then he cried out in fear as something slithered over his shoe and plucked at his ankle. He started back, and looked down. It was a hand. A ledge of earth, inches wide, ran along the other side of the fence and crumbled away to the rock face a few feet below: then the drop was sheer to the tarn-like water. The hand now clutched at the ledge.

From *The Moon of Gomrath* by Alan Garner

Thinking back

Rearrange these sentences to retell the main points of the passage.
Something grabbed Colin's ankle.
Colin woke up and discovered Susan's bed was empty.
Colin ran to the edge of the cliff but could not see Susan.
Colin looked down and saw a hand clutching a ledge.
Susan was sleep-walking towards the quarry.

Thinking about it

1 What do you think woke Colin?
2 Why couldn't Colin understand how Susan had got out?
3 How did Colin realise it was Susan?
4 What was the countryside like near their house?
5 How can you tell Colin could see clearly, even though it was at night?
6 Why didn't Colin shout to warn Susan?
7 Whose hand do you think it was? Why?

Thinking it through

1 How can you tell Colin was really worried?
2 What words and phrases does the writer use to tell you Colin was in a hurry?
3 What thoughts would have gone through Colin's mind when he found Susan's bed empty?
4 What do these words mean? (Use a dictionary if you are unsure.) a) silhouette b) quarry c) tarn
5 Did you find the passage exciting? Why?
6 What did you like about the way the author wrote?
7 When a story ends at an exciting point, it is often called a 'cliff-hanger'. This passage is a 'cliff-hanger' in two different ways. Why?

UNIT 3   The Hairy Toe

Think ahead

Do you think this is going to be a story or a poem? Why?

Once there was a woman who went out to pick beans,
and she found a Hairy Toe.
She took the Hairy Toe home with her,
and that night, when she went to bed,
the wind began to moan and groan.
Away in the distance
she seemed to hear a voice crying,
'Where's my Hair-r-ry To-o-oe?'
'Who's got my Hair-r-ry To-o-oe?'

The woman scrooched down
under the covers
and pulled them tight around her head.
The wind growled around her house
like some big animal
and r-r-rumbled
over the chimbley.
All at once she heard the door cr-r-a-ack
and Something slipped in
and began to creep over the floor.
The floor went
cre-e-eak, cre-e-eak
at every step the thing took towards her bed.
The woman could almost feel
it bending over her bed.
Then in an awful voice it said:
'Where's my Hair-r-ry To-o-oe?'
'Who's got my Hair-r-ry To-o-oe?'
YOU'VE GOT IT!'

Anon (traditional American)

Thinking back

Choose the best words to finish each sentence.
1 The woman found   a) a hairy foot   b) a hairy toe
2 The wind began to   a) whisper   b) moan and groan
3 The woman was   a) in the bath   b) in bed
4 The woman thought she heard   a) a voice   b) a footstep
5 Something began to   a) creep over the floor   b) snore
6 The woman could almost feel the thing:
   a) bending over her bed   b) crawling under her bed

 Thinking about it

1 Why do you think the woman took the Hairy Toe home with her? Do you think that was sensible?
2 How can you tell the woman was scared by the voice?
3 What do you think the 'Something' that slipped into the house might have been?
4 How do you think the 'Something' spoke? How did its voice sound?
5 How could the poem carry on? Say what you think happened.

 Thinking it through

1 Could this *really* have happened? Explain your answer.
2 Someone has explained the poem by saying 'At night, our thoughts sometimes play tricks on us.'
   What do you think the person meant?
3 Is this poem best read or spoken? Give your reasons.
4 Name something that you think is 'special' about this poem and say why.
5 Name some things:
   a) it is sensible to be scared of. Say why.
   b) it is foolish to be scared of. Say why.

UNIT 4   The Professor and the Ferryman

Think ahead

What is a professor? What is a ferryman? Who is the wiser?

Is there a difference between wisdom and learning?

There was once an old ferryman who ferried people across the River Ganges in his boat. The ferryman was not wealthy or educated, but he never grumbled. He loved his job because he never had to hurry and had plenty of time to think.

One day a very well-dressed man carrying a briefcase came by. As they were crossing the river the man said, 'Have you ever studied science?'

'No, sir. I haven't,' the ferryman replied. 'I have never been to school and never learned to read or write.'

The man was taken back with surprise. 'What!' he exclaimed. 'Never studied science? Don't you know anything? I am a scientist. Scientists are the most important people in the world.'

The ferryman looked sad. He had never been made to feel so stupid or foolish before. He felt worthless.

Just then the sky darkened and black clouds gathered. The wind got up and the boat began to rock alarmingly. There was a distant roar of thunder. Rapidly the weather worsened. The waves got stronger and bigger and suddenly the boat began to sink. 'We'll have to swim for it,' shouted the ferryman.

The scientist clutched his briefcase fearfully. 'Oh dear. I cannot swim. I never learnt!' he cried.

Just then both men were swept into the raging water. The old ferryman swam slowly to the shore and dragged himself, wet and shivering, onto the river bank. But the scientist, still clutching his important briefcase, sank and disappeared beneath the waters of the Ganges.

Thinking back

Copy and complete each sentence with a suitable word.

1 The ferryman carried people across the ____ in his boat.
2 One day a ____ wanted to cross the river.
3 The man carried a ____ .
4 The man asked the ferryman if he had ever studied ____ .
5 The ferryman explained that he had never been to ____ .
6 The man told the ferryman that he was a ____ .
7 Suddenly the weather got ____ .
8 The boat began to ____ .

Thinking about it

1 How do you know the story took place in India?
2 List things you know about the ferryman.
3 Why did the ferryman like his job?
4 List some things you know about the professor.
5 Do you think the ferryman really knew nothing about science? Explain your answer.
6 What do you think happened at the end of the story?

Thinking it through

1 Was the scientist a likeable man? Give your reasons.
2 The ferryman said he felt 'worthless'. Why did he? What does this mean?
3 Who do you think was the wiser – the ferryman or the scientist? Give your reasons.
4 What lesson can we learn from this story?
5 Where do we learn most – at home or school? Explain your answer.

UNIT 5 Robin Hood gets a Ducking

Think ahead

Who was Robin Hood? What do you know about him?

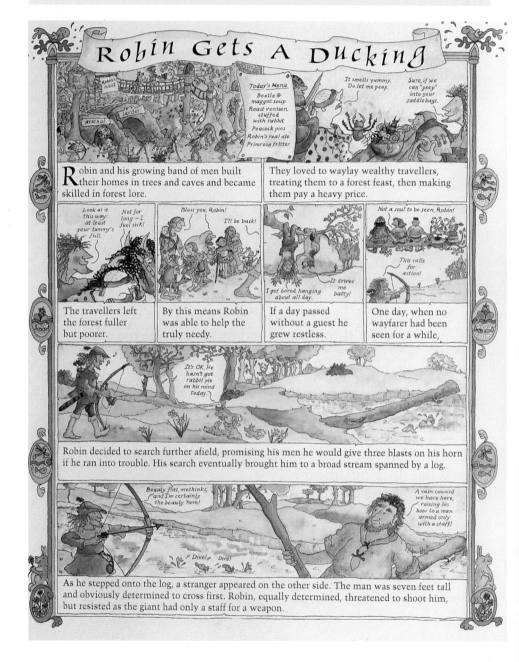

Robin Gets A Ducking

Robin and his growing band of men built their homes in trees and caves and became skilled in forest lore.

They loved to waylay wealthy travellers, treating them to a forest feast, then making them pay a heavy price.

The travellers left the forest fuller but poorer.

By this means Robin was able to help the truly needy.

If a day passed without a guest he grew restless.

One day, when no wayfarer had been seen for a while,

Robin decided to search further afield, promising his men he would give three blasts on his horn if he ran into trouble. His search eventually brought him to a broad stream spanned by a log.

As he stepped onto the log, a stranger appeared on the other side. The man was seven feet tall and obviously determined to cross first. Robin, equally determined, threatened to shoot him, but resisted as the giant had only a staff for a weapon.

12

13

Thinking back

Match the endings to the sentence beginnings. Write the correct sentences in your book.
1 Robin Hood and his men — to the poor.
2 Robin gave money — lived in the forest.
3 A tall stranger tried to cross a log bridge — made friends.
4 The giant knocked Robin — at the same time as Robin.
5 The tall stranger and Robin — into the water.

 Thinking about it

1 'The travellers left the forest fuller but poorer.' Explain what this means.
2 Why was Robin loved by the poor?
3 How can you tell Robin liked to fight fairly?
4 Is it true to say that Robin and the stranger were evenly matched when they fought? Give your reasons.
5 Why did Robin give three blasts on his horn?
6 How can you tell the tall stranger and Robin liked each other?

 Thinking it through

1 What clues are there that tell you the story took place long ago?
2 Many stories about Robin Hood may be myths. What does this mean?
3 Say what you think each of the following means:
   a) outlaw b) waylay c) gave an inch
   d) stayed their hands
4 How helpful are the pictures? How do they add to your understanding of the story?

UNIT 6   The Great Escape

Think ahead

Read the title and look at the picture. What do you think the story is about? Now read the introduction to the story. Does this give you any more clues?

Lubber, a stray dog, was found wandering homeless. He was put in a Dogs' Home, but as no-one has claimed him after two weeks, he is about to be put to sleep. Squintum, the vet's cat, helps him escape.

'Run for it!' squalled Squintum at the top of his awful voice. 'Follow me, or else they'll kill you!'

Lubber was not the most quick-witted of dogs, and the full meaning of Squintum's final words hadn't really dawned upon him. But he had been trained, from a puppy, to respond to simple commands, and now he had received two – to run for it and to follow the cat – and he obeyed. With one mighty leap, he was off the table and out of the surgery door. Behind him, the vet and the kennel maid stood open-mouthed. On the floor, knocked off by a passing blow from Lubber's shaven foreleg, lay the syringe.

Along the corridor raced Squintum, and into the kennel block. Unlike the inmates of the Dogs' Home, who knew only their prison cells, Squintum knew every inch of the place.

Now, like all their kind, the dogs in the kennel block grew wildly excited as Squintum sped down the central passage between their cages, followed, at his best speed, by the lumbering Lubber.

On ran the Siamese, the bloodthirsty cries dying away behind him, through the office, through the Manager's sitting room, through the kitchen, making for the back door. Behind him Lubber galloped wildly, swerving round corners, sliding on polished floors, skidding on rugs, knocking over little tables bearing little ornaments that broke into little pieces, intent only on following the cat as he had been told.

Squintum was the most quick-witted of cats, but on this occasion, not quick enough. Intent only on saving the dog's life, he had forgotten the difference in their sizes.

The back door of the Dogs' Home was a glass-panelled one, with a metal cat flap set in the bottom of it, through which went Squintum with the ease of long practice and the speed of light. Passers-by in the street outside saw a lean cream-coloured cat with a dark face and legs come shooting out of the cat flap, and then they jumped back in startled surprise.

With a shattering crash, the glass-panelled back door of the Dogs' Home exploded in a thousand shards and splinters, as through it, as easily as if it had been a paper hoop in a circus ring, burst a large, hairy dog.

From *Find the White Horse* by Dick King-Smith

 Thinking back

Copy these sentences. Think of a suitable word to fill in each gap.

The vet was just about to put Lubber to __1__. Squintum the __2__ told Lubber to run for it and to __3__ him. Lubber __4__ after Squintum. The other dogs grew very __5__ when they saw them running away. Lubber slid on the __6__ floors and skidded on the __7__. Squintum went through the cat __8__ in the back door. Lubber was too __9__ to get through the cat flap so he burst through the __10__ in the door with a crash.

Thinking about it

1 How long did the Dog's Home keep stray dogs before they put them to sleep?
2 Look carefully for information about Lubber and Squintum. Write five things you can discover about each of them. Do it like this:

Lubber	Squintum
Lubber was a big hairy dog.	Squintum was the vet's cat

3 How can you tell the vet and kennel maid were surprised when Lubber jumped off the table?
4 How did Squintum know 'every inch' of the Dog's Home?
5 How can you tell Lubber was rather a big, clumsy dog?
6 How did the passers-by react when Lubber came crashing through the back door?

Thinking it through

1 What feelings do you have for Lubber after reading the passage?
2 Why do you think we say 'put to sleep' and not 'kill'. Do they mean the same?
3 Was the vet being cruel in trying to put Lubber to sleep? Give your reasons.
4 Are you pleased Lubber escaped? Explain why.
5 Find these words and phrases in the passage. Explain what they mean:
a) squalled   b) quick-witted   c) exploded in a thousand shards and splinters
6 What do you think this saying means – 'A dog is for life, not just Christmas'?

Think ahead

Think of three things you already know about foxes.
This extract will tell you many more things!

EDITOR'S PAGE

The Red Fox

The Red Fox is dog-like in appearance. It has pointed ears, a narrow muzzle and a bushy, white-tipped tail. The Red Fox measures about 120 cm in length and has a shoulder height of up to 40 cm. A fully grown fox weighs approximately 10 kg. Its colour is usually reddish brown with a white chest and stomach.

The presence of a fox may be detected by its tracks, the scattered remains of food around its den, a distinctive musty smell, and long twisted droppings containing hair, bone and insect remains.

The Red Fox is found throughout Europe. It lives in a variety of habitats, usually in places where there is plenty of cover. In many places it ventures into villages and towns for food.

The fox is a carnivore (meat-eater), whose diet

consists mainly of rodents but a variety of larger animals and fruit are eaten. Animals who live in or near towns often scavenge for food.

Last week we ran the above article on Red Foxes.
During the week I received a post-bag full of letters about foxes. I have printed just a few of them here.

Dear Editor
Foxes are a pest. They steal chickens from farms and raid dustbins in towns. They serve no useful purpose and should be destroyed.
Yours faithfully
(No name or address supplied)

Dear Editor
I believe that all life should be protected and that it is unnecessary to kill foxes. Nature has her own ways of controlling the population of all creatures. Nature does not need our help. Leave foxes alone!
Signed
Mrs D Duckworth

Dear Editor
There are too many foxes, which means that they cause a nuisance to farmers and townsfolk alike. Hunting them provides harmless sport for many. It provides a good day for the hounds and the hunters and is not unnecessarily cruel to the foxes. Did you know that in fact more foxes are killed on the roads than by hunting? Less than 20% of foxes are hunted – so what's all the fuss about?

Mr G Kirkham, Master of the Ferrydown Hunt

Dear Editor
Imagine you are out in the country minding your own business when suddenly you are set upon and chased by a pack of bloodthirsty baying hounds who are intent on ripping you to pieces. The deafening thunder of horse's hooves and the bray of bugles rings in your ears. You run as fast as you can until you are dropping with exhaustion. How would you feel? Hunting is harmless to foxes? You must be joking!

Signed
Yours disgustedly
Mr Ben Harris

 Thinking back

Copy and complete this chart.

FACTS ABOUT THE RED FOX	
Length	
Height	
Weight	
Distinctive features	
Name of home	
Food eaten	
Usual habitat	

Thinking about it

1 Where did the article on foxes appear? How do you know?
2 Why do you think the editor was surprised to get such a response to the article?
3 What are all four letters about?
4 Why do you think the first letter was not signed?
5 Which letters are in favour of hunting foxes?
6 Which two people are against fox hunting?
7 Why do you think Mr Harris signs his letter in the way he does?
8 Why do you think Mr Kirkham explains who he is at the end of his letter?

 Thinking it through

1 Copy one of the letters in favour of fox hunting and one against it. Underline all the key words, phrases or sentences in each letter that are trying to persuade you of the writer's point of view.
2 Which letter uses some facts and figures to try and persuade you?
3 Draw a chart in your book. List some of the arguments in favour of fox hunting and those against it, that are stated in the letters. Do it like this:

Views in favour of fox hunting	Views against fox hunting

UNIT 8 An Interview

Think ahead

What do you want to be when you grow up? Have you ever thought of becoming a pop star?

QUESTION: *How did you become a pop star?*

ANSWER: Since I was about 12, I've wanted to sing. I used to watch my favourite bands on TV and mime to them! I asked for a guitar for a birthday present and worked hard to learn to play it. Then, when I was at college, a few friends and I with similar interests got

Gary Goldwater is a singer in a pop band.

together and started a band. We would play at parties for nothing! Then someone said we were very good. They said we should turn professional. So we got ourselves a manager and started playing in clubs – and we got paid for it!

QUESTION: *Tell me about your first real show.*

ANSWER: Our first big show was a real nightmare! Our van broke down and we arrived very late. We didn't have much time to set things up and one of the microphones packed up. Rod, the drummer, lost one of his drumsticks and I knocked an amplifier over. To top all that, during our act the electricity went and so we were all plunged into darkness. In spite of all that, we survived! The crowds were really great.

QUESTION: *What is your most exciting memory?*

ANSWER: Flying across the Atlantic in Concorde! The band was

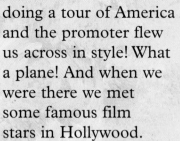

doing a tour of America and the promoter flew us across in style! What a plane! And when we were there we met some famous film stars in Hollywood.

QUESTION: *What is life as a pop star really like?*

ANSWER: It's good fun, but it's really hard work. You have to spend alot of time on the road, travelling to different shows. You have to be able to take a lot of knocks and put up with lots of disappointments. Learning to play the guitar is not as easy as it looks. It takes a lot of time and a lot of practice.

Equipping a band is very expensive – musical instruments are not cheap. You also need a lot of luck and a good manager – there are a lot of unscrupulous people in show business. You need to be very single-minded and dedicated. So, it's not an easy life, but I love it!

Thinking back

1 Who is the article about ?
2 What is Gary?
3 Where did Gary form his first band?
4 Was Gary's first real show easy or difficult?
5 What is Gary's most exciting memory?
6 What does Gary say about equipping a band?

Thinking about it

1 Explain why Gary found his first show difficult.
2 Why was the visit to America so memorable?
3 Why do you think Gary says dedication is important?
4 Why do you think being a pop star could be expensive?
5 What do the following mean:
   a) mime   b) turning professional
   c) amplify   d) unscrupulous?

Thinking it through

1 Do you think being a pop star is boring? Give your reasons.
2 Gary loves his job, but all jobs have their ups and downs. Copy this chart and think of five points for each column.

Being a pop star	
Good things	Things that are not so good

3 What is the purpose of an interview?
4 What skills do you think an interviewer needs?

UNIT 9   It Was Long Ago

Think ahead

What is the earliest memory you have?

I dragged on the dusty road, and I remember
How the old woman looked over the fence at me
And seemed to know

How it felt to be three, and called out, I remember,
'Do you like bilberries and cream for tea?'
I went under the tree

And while she hummed, and the cat purred, I remember
How she filled a saucer with berries and cream for me
So long ago,

Such berries and such cream I remember
I had never seen before, and may never see
Today, you know.

And that is almost all I can remember,
The house, the mountain, the grey cat on her knee,
Her red shawl, and the tree.

And the taste of the berries and the feel of the sun I remember,
And the smell of everything that used to be
So long ago.

Till the heat on the road outside again I remember,
And how the long dusty road seemed to have for me
No end, you know.

That is the farthest I can remember.
It won't mean much to you. It does to me.
Then I grew up, you see.

From *It Was Long Ago* by Eleanor Farjeon

Thinking back

1 What was the road like?
2 How old was the poet at the time of the memory?
3 What did the old woman call out?
4 What did the cat do while the old woman prepared the berries and cream?
5 What was the old woman wearing?

Thinking about it

1 What do you think 'long ago' means?
2 What a) sounds b) tastes c) smells can the poet remember?
3 What clues are there in the poem that tell you it was hot?
4 Why did the long dusty road 'seem to have no end' do you think?
5 Why do you think this memory meant so much to the poet?

Thinking it through

1 What could the last line of the poem mean?
2 What makes you remember some things and not others?
3 Write your earliest happy memory. Why do you think this means so much to you?
4 Why do you think old people like to talk about their memories?

UNIT 10   Snow White in New York

Think ahead

How can you tell that this is not going to be the traditional version of Snow White, even before you read the story?

Once upon a time in New York there was a poor little rich girl called Snow White. Her mother was dead and for a while she lived happily with her father. But one day he married again …

All the papers said Snow White's stepmother was the classiest dame in New York. But no-one knew she was Queen of the Underworld. She liked to see herself in the *New York Mirror*. But one day she read something to make her very jealous – 'Snow White the Belle of New York City' – and she plotted to get rid of her stepdaughter.

'Take her down and shoot her,' she said to one of her bodyguards.

The man took Snow White deep into the dark streets, but he could not do it. He left her there, lost and alone.

Snow White wandered the streets all night, tired and hungry. In the early morning she heard music coming from an open door. She went inside.

The seven jazz-men were sorry for her. 'Stay here if you like,' they said, 'but you'll have to work.'

'What can I do?' she asked.

'Can you sing?' asked one of them.

The very first night Snow White sang there was a reporter in the club. He knew at once that she would be a star.

26

Next day Snow White was on the front page of the *New York Mirror*. The stepmother was mad with rage. 'This time I shall get rid of her myself,' she said.

And so she decided to hold a grand party in honour of Snow White's success ... but ... secretly she dropped a poisoned cherry in a cocktail and handed it to Snow White with a smile.

All New York was shocked by the death of the beautiful Snow White.

Crowds of people stood in the rain and watched Snow White's coffin pass by.

The seven jazz-men, their hearts broken, carried the coffin unsteadily up the church steps. Suddenly one of them stumbled, and, to everyone's amazement, Snow White opened her eyes.

The first person she saw was the reporter.

He smiled at her and she smiled back.

The poisoned cherry that had been stuck in her throat was gone. She was alive.

Snow White and the reporter fell in love. They had a big society wedding, and the next day cruised off on a glorious honeymoon together.

From *Snow White in New York* by Fiona French

 Thinking back

Copy these sentences that tell the story. Fill in the gaps with suitable words.
Snow White _1_ in New York. One day her father got _2_ again. Snow White's stepmother was very _3_ of her. She told one of her _4_ to _5_ Snow White. He took her into the dark streets and _6_ her there. Seven _7_ told Snow White she would be safe with them. When Snow White _8_ at the club a _9_ saw her. The stepmother saw a _10_ of Snow White in the New York _11_. She _12_ a party in _13_ of Snow White. She tried to _14_ Snow White by putting a _15_ cherry in her drink.

Thinking about it

1 The author says 'Snow White was a *poor* little *rich* girl.' What does this mean? How could she be both poor and rich?
2 Snow White's stepmother was Queen of the Underworld. What do you think this means?
3 Was the New York Mirror really a mirror? How can you tell?
4 Why was the stepmother jealous of Snow White?
5 Where did the seven jazz-men work?
6 How did Snow White get her picture on the front page of a newspaper?
7 After all her stepmother had done, why do you think Snow White agreed to go to her party?
8 How did Snow White come 'back to life'?

 Thinking it through

1 What did you think of the story? Did you like it? Name some things you liked or did not like about it.
2 In what ways could you describe the story as clever?
3 List some of the similarities and differences between this version of the story and the more well-known version.
4 In what way did the story have a fairy-tale beginning and ending?
5 The story doesn't tell us what happened to the step-mother. Write a paragraph on what you think happened.

UNIT 11   Once Upon a Time ...

Think ahead

Once upon a time ... What sort of a story do you expect when you hear these words?

Common story themes

Throughout the world, for thousands of years, stories have been told and passed on from generation to generation by word of mouth. These traditional stories often have common themes like the struggle between good and evil, rich and poor, young and old, beautiful and ugly, male and female. The common ingredients of such stories are things like magic and the supernatural, heroes and villains, animals behaving like humans, epic journeys and so on.

Collecting traditional stories

Gradually, stories were written down. One of the earliest collections of such stories was compiled a thousand years ago in India by Somadeva, a Brahmin, or wise man, from Kashmir. In Europe, many traditional tales were first written down by an Italian called Charles Perrault, in the 17th century. These included stories like Sleeping Beauty and Red Riding Hood. Many versions of well-loved stories that we know today, like Hansel and Gretel, were collected by two German brothers, Jacob and Wilhelm Grimm, in the 18th century.

'Travelling' stories

Similar stories are often told all over the world. They must have been carried round the world by travellers. The story of Snow White crops up in different forms all over the world. The version most of us know is that told by the 1938 Walt Disney film.

Thinking back

1 List some common themes in traditional stories.
2 List some common ingredients in traditional stories.
3 How were stories passed on before books?
4 Who made the first collection of stories?
5 Name the first Italian and German collectors of traditional stories.

Thinking about it

1 Explain how the same stories travelled from country to country in the past.
2 Why do you think the story of Snow White varies in different countries?
3 Why do you think we know the Walt Disney version of Snow White best?
4 Name as many traditional tales and fairy stories as possible.

Thinking it through

1 Why do you think fairy stories are so popular?
2 Copy this chart. Think of as many fairy stories as possible to help you complete it.

Good characters	Bad characters

3 List some typical settings found in fairy stories such as palaces, forests.
4 Name a fairy story which contains:
a) a journey   b) animals who can talk and behave like humans   c) a monster   d) some form of magic

UNIT 12　How Laughter Helped Stop the Argument

Think ahead

What sort of things cause arguments? How do you solve arguments – by persuasion? laughter? some other way?

First Voice:　*Look at the clouds*
so fluffy
so sheepy
That's because God
got woolly hair.

Second voice:　*Look at the rain*
falling in strands
falling everywhere.
That's because God
got straight hair.

Third voice:　*Look at de sun*
look at de moon
That's why
God got a yellow eye.

Fourth voice:　*Look at the sea*
look at the sky
That's a clue
God's skin must be blue.

Fifth voice:　*What about the night*
that wraps us dark
and makes us sleep tight?
God's skin must be black.

Sixth voice:	*What about the snow?*
	Oh no, God's skin must be white.
Third voice:	*No, God's skin must be green*
	look at de trees
	See what I mean.
First voice:	*Well, then since you are all so clever*
	just answer me
	Is God a father or a mother?
Second voice:	*A father.*
Fifth voice:	*A mother.*
Sixth voice:	*No, a father.*
Third voice:	*How about a grandmother?*

AND WHILE THESE SIX VOICES
WERE ARGUING AND ARGUING
JUST THEN A SEVENTH VOICE STEPPED
IN

Listen my friends
and listen well
crick me your ears
and I'll crack you a spell
God might be a story with no beginning
and no end

God might be laughter
for all you know
God might be   a HA - HA - HA - HAaaaaaaaaaaaa
*   a HO - HO - HO - HOoooooooooooo*
*   a HE - HE - HE - HEeeeeeeeeeeee*
*   a SHE - SHE - SHE - SHEeeeeeeeeeeee*

a million million
*   laughing pebbles*
*   inside of*
*   you and me.*

That's what God might be.

From *Laughter in an Egg* by John Agard

32

Thinking back

Complete each sentence.
1 The first person said that God must have woolly hair because _____ .
2 The second person said that God must have straight hair because _____ .
3 The fifth person said that God must be black because _____ .
4 The sixth person said that God must be white because _____ .

 Thinking about it

1 Which people thought God was a man?
2 Which people thought God was a woman?
3 Why do you think all of the people are finding it hard to describe God?
4 What does the seventh person think God might be like?
5 Who's view of God do you prefer? Say why.

Thinking it through

1 How can you tell this is a poem and not a play?
2 In what ways is this poem set out like a play?
3 If you were the narrator (storyteller) and had to set the scene for the poem what would you say?
4 There are some clues in the language of the poem that it is written by someone from the West Indies. Copy some of the evidence and explain what it tells you.
5 Which parts of the text are written:
   a) in italic print? Why?
   b) in capital letters? Why?
6 Write what you thought of the poem.

UNIT 13   How to make an Identi-kit Flick Book

Think ahead

What is an identi-kit picture? Who uses such pictures?

You will need:
- eight sheets of A4 paper   • a stapler   • a ruler
- a pair of scissors   • pens and pencils for drawing/colouring

What you do:

Step 1 Staple the eight pieces of paper together.

Step 2 Design the cover for your book.

Step 3 Measure each inside page into equal strips of the same depth.

Step 4 Cut each inside page into four equal strips. NB DON'T CUT THE FRONT OR BACK COVERS!

Step 5 Look carefully at the diagram which shows you what each strip is for.

Step 6 Draw a face on the first inside page of your book.

Step 7 Draw a different face on each page of your book.

Step 8 Have fun making different faces by turning back different strips from different pages.

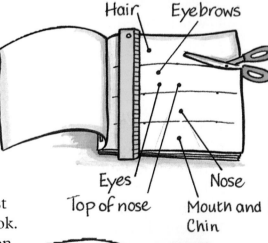

Hair   Eyebrows

Eyes   Nose

Top of nose   Mouth and Chin

Points to remember
- Include men's and women's faces.
- Make them as varied as possible.
- Include things like earrings, glasses, hair styles, scars.
- Make the eyes, noses and mouths different shapes.
- Remember that men sometimes have moustaches and beards!

 Thinking back

Answer these questions with sensible sentences.
1 What are the instructions for?
2 What five things do you need before you can begin?
3 How many steps are there in the process?
4 What warning is given in Step 4?
5 How many points are listed under 'Points to Remember'?

 Thinking about it

1 At what step do you need the stapler?
2 At what step do you need the ruler?
3 At what step do you need the scissors?
4 At which steps do you do any drawing?
5 Why do you have to draw a different face on every page?
6 How do you make different identi-kit faces with your book?

 Thinking it through

1 a) Why does the 'You will need' section come first?
  b) Why is each item in the list bullet-pointed?
2 a) How clear were the instructions?
  b) What made them easy to follow?
  c) How helpful are the diagrams?
3 Why are some things written in capital letters?

UNIT 14   Pandora's Box

Think ahead

In the Greek myth, Pandora was told not to open the box.
Do you think she will?

In the beginning there were no such things as old age, sickness, greed and envy. Prometheus shut up all these nasty things in a box. He gave the box to his brother Epimetheus. He told him that the box was not to be opened.

Everything on Earth was lovely – except for one thing. They had no fire. One day Prometheus stole some from heaven. This made Jupiter, the king of the gods, so angry that he decided to punish Prometheus and the other humans.

Jupiter made a woman called Pandora. She was very beautiful but she was also very foolish and mischievous. Jupiter sent her to Epimetheus as a gift. Epimetheus didn't really trust this gift from the gods so he made Pandora promise never to open the box. But of course she was very foolish and, just as the gods had planned, her curiosity got the better of her. One day, Pandora was sure she could hear voices inside calling out to her, 'Please let us out!'

Pandora lifted the lid slowly and carefully to peep in. As she did so there was a whoosh! and all the horrible things that had been trapped inside escaped – illness, unhappiness, sadness, crimes and so on. They flew out of the box and out through the open windows into the world. Pandora quickly tried to shut the box but only managed to trap one small bright shining sprite inside. This was Hope – all that was left to encourage people in an evil world.

Thinking back

Match up the beginnings and endings of these sentences. Write the sentences correctly in your book.

1 Prometheus trapped nasty things	as a gift.
2 Prometheus gave the box	Hope.
3 Jupiter sent Pandora to Epimetheus	the box.
4 Pandora promised not to open	to escape.
5 Pandora broke	in a box.
6 Pandora allowed the nasty things	her promise.
7 The only thing left in the box was	to Epimetheus.

 Thinking about it

1 Write what sort of character you think each of the following were. Give your reasons.
   a) Prometheus   b) Epimetheus   c) Jupiter
2 Why did Prometheus steal some fire from heaven?
3 What effect did this have on Jupiter?
4 Why didn't Epimetheus trust a gift from the gods?
5 What can you learn about Pandora from the story?

 Thinking it through

1 What more could Epimetheus have done to prevent Pandora from opening the box?
2 In what way are each of the following characters responsible for the nastiness in the world:
   a) Pandora b) Epimetheus c) Prometheus d) Jupiter?
3 What do you think the last sentence of the story means?
4 Can we learn any lessons from this story today?

UNIT 15 The Magic Box

Think ahead

*Inside Pandora's Box (Unit 14) were all sorts of nasty things.
Inside this box are all sorts of nice things. Before you read the
poem, guess what things the poet might have chosen to go in his
'magic' box.*

I will put into that box
the swish of a silk sari on a summer night
fire from the nostrils of a Chinese dragon,
the tip of a tongue touching a tooth.

I will put into the box
a snowman with a rumbling belly,
a sip of the bluest water from lake Lucerne,
a leaping spark from an electric fish.

I will put into the box
three violet wishes spoken in Gujarati,
the last joke of an ancient uncle,
and the first smile of a baby.

I will put into the box
a fifth season and a black sun,
a cowboy on a broomstick
and a witch on a white horse.

My box is fashioned from ice and gold and steel,
with stars on the lid and secrets in the corner.
Its hinges are the toe joints
of dinosaurs.

I shall surf in my box
on the great high-rolling breakers of the wild Atlantic,
then wash ashore on a yellow beach
the colour of the sun.

From *Cat Among the Pigeons* by Kit Wright

Thinking back

1 If SSSSN = the swish of a silk sari on a summer night, what would these mean?
   a) FNCD b) SRB c) LSEF d) LJAU e) FSB f) WWH
2 What will be spoken in Gujarati?
3 Describe how the box is made.
4 Describe the beach the poet will land on.

Thinking about it

1 What is Gujarati?
2 How could you 'capture' the first smile of a baby?
3 a) What name would you give to a fifth season?
   b) What would the weather be like in your fifth season?
4 Which of the things in the box do you think are real and which are imaginary?

Thinking it through

1 In what way is the poem about magic?
2 What is your favourite thing in the box? Why?
3 What is the most strange thing the poet will put in the box? Why?
4 What do you think is special about this poem?
5 Is wishing the same as wanting? Explain what you think.

Think ahead

Look carefully at the Greek News.
Do you think it is a present-day newspaper?

MORE SCHOOL?

People think of Greece as a centre of great learning. Yet most of our children can't even read and write! The Greek News asks *you*, the readers, if more boys should be sent to school.

❦AGAINST SCHOOL❦

Frankly, most of you thought education was a waste of time and money. The following examples give a pretty clear idea of your replies:

'Only rich families can afford to send their sons to school or to buy a well-educated slave to teach them. How many of us have got the money to do that?'

'What use is school in later life? A boy should be learning about his father's trade, whether it's farming, mending shoes or making pottery.'

'It's madness to send a boy off to school at 7 years old. That's just when he's starting to be useful around the farm or in the workshop.'

❦FOR SCHOOL❦

It was only the wealthiest amongst you who had anything good to say about education. The following view was typical:

'Education sets our sons apart from the common people.

And they need to go to school until they are 18 years old. It takes at least seven or eight years just to beat some basic learning into them – reading and writing, sums, music, athletics, that sort of thing.

Only when a boy is 15 or 16 years old is he ready to be taught some of the higher arts, such as learning how to speak cleverly in public. With this skill, he can help his family gain more power in the Assembly.

Mind you, there's not much point in educating every boy. Reading and writing's not much use on the farm now, is it!'

So, as with many things in life, it all seems to depend on how much money you have.

GIRLS TOO?

Should girls be taught to read and write? What did *you*, the public, think?

'OH, NO,' seemed to be the answer, 'most definitely not!'

Many of you felt there was no point in educating girls. They need to learn things like spinning, weaving and cooking, in order to run a household smoothly once they are married. And the best place to learn these skills is at home with their mothers!

A few rich parents said they would let their daughters learn to read, but only from a slave at home – never by going out to school.

HAVE YOUR SAY.

ere is this week's tter to the Editor. If ou have a complaint or ripe, why not write to e? (Ed.)

ear Editor

am sick and tired of omplaining! Nothing ver seems to get done!

I have lived in Athens or 30 years and life in he city has gradually got worse and worse. I have several complaints.

Firstly our streets are ittered with people's rubbish, which smells, spreads disease and encourages rats. When are we going to get a proper collection system going?

Secondly, when are we going to get some proper building regulations? The city is becoming overcrowded. No-one seems to care about where people build or what state their buildings are in. It's disgraceful!

Thirdly, because of this higgledy-piggledy growth our streets are narrow and twisty. They provide ideal places for thieves and crooks to hang around. I no longer feel safe in my own city. This is no way to live or to bring up a family. Let's have some action NOW – before it's too late!

 Yours faithfully
 Demetrius Milo

PROPERTY CORNER

❧ FOR SALE ❧

DELIGHTFUL HOUSE IN THE COUNTRY

Spacious rooms surround a large courtyard with altar to household gods. Accommodation includes luxurious men's 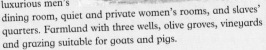 dining room, quiet and private women's rooms, and slaves' quarters. Farmland with three wells, olive groves, vineyards and grazing suitable for goats and pigs.

2 KILOMETRES WEST OF DELPHI

NEW ON THE MARKET

Lampmaker's shop and house, opens onto busy street with lots of passing trade. Plastered brick walls and clay tiled roof in good condition. Large house has kitchen, dining room and store rooms. Plenty of work space in courtyard beside shop. Close to a public fountain and near to the harbour – ideal for shipping goods to foreign markets.

LAMPMAKERS' DISTRICT, EPHESOS

Thinking back

1 Did most people think school was a good or bad idea for boys?
2 Write two of the reasons given against school.
3 Write one reason given for sending boys to school.
4 List some of the subjects that were taught to boys who went to school.
5 Why did most people think there was no point in educating girls?
6 Which of the following things did Demetrius Milo complain about: rubbish in the streets; overcrowding; the noise from the market; poor buildings; safety in the city; the lack of museums?
7 How does the advert describe the house near Delphi?

Thinking about it

1 Did all children go to school? Explain your answer.
2 What sort of jobs did boys do, who didn't go to school?
3 What sort of families did send their children to school?
4 Why do you think these families thought 'speaking cleverly in public' was so important?
5 Do you think that most people felt 'a woman's place is in the home'? Say why.
6 What skills did people think girls needed to learn.
7 Why wasn't Demetrius Milo hopeful anything would be done about the things he was asking for?
8 What changes did he request?
9 In what ways are the two houses that are advertised different from each other?

Thinking it through

1 After reading the section on 'Education Issues' say which point of view you agree with and why.
2 How was the education system in Ancient Greece different from the way we educate children today?
3 Do you think the education system in Greece was fair? Give your reasons.
4 The letter of complaint is a mixture of facts and opinions. Write down what facts you can learn from Demetrius Milo's letter, such as: The streets are littered with rubbish.
5 Advertisements usually only tell you the good things and leave out the bad things. For example, the house near Delphi is near a smelly marsh. The farmer in the next farm is a miserable old man. The roof tiles need replacing and the vines in the vineyard have a disease! Write some of the things that might not be so good about the house in Ephesos.

UNIT 17 Reporting the News

Think ahead

What is news? How does the news we see on TV get to us?

How news is collected

1 There is a motorway pile-up in fog.

2 The local police and fire brigade are soon on the scene.

3 A local reporter arrives soon after.

4 It is a big story. The local reporter tells the national television companies.

5 The TV companies send their own reporter and camera team to the scene. The team have to drop everything and leave immediately.

6 As soon as they arrive they have to find out as much as possible, as quickly as possible.

7 The team file their first report and send it back immediately.

8 The television company's news centre receives the report and starts to work on it.

9 The editor reads the report, along with the other day's news, to decide whether to show it on TV or not.

10 The report is shown on the evening news.

A day in the life of a news editor

A news editor kept a diary for a day at work, explaining how a news programme is made.

I arrived in the office at 6.30 this morning as I had a lot work to do. The first thing I did was to listen to the news on Radio 4 and read all the morning papers. News stories arrive all the time by phone, fax and satellite and I had to keep my eye on those as well.

My boss, the main editor, arrived at work at 9.30am. Immediately we had a meeting about which stories we wanted to cover. When we had made our decision the editor told the news crews which stories they had to cover.

I grabbed a quick lunch with another news editor at 12pm – no time to waste!

Back in the office for another meeting at 1.30pm about the day's main news stories. Now we had to start deciding which items we would feature in the news programme.

We had another meeting at 3pm! This time we discussed which items we are going to have in tomorrow's programme.

At 5pm we made the final decision about which stories were going to be on the news and which order they would be in. However, we have to be prepared to make changes to the running order at the last minute, because if a big story breaks we have to feature it and drop something else.

The studio director was really busy at 5.45 as she got everything ready in the studio for the broadcast.

6pm: The news programme went on air!

I went home around 7pm, exhausted but looking forward to another exciting day in the office.

AGENDA FOR 1.30 MEETING

1 Consider current news items

2 Decide which to include in 6 o'clock news

3 Put items in rough order

4 Check incoming news items

Thinking back

1 Who were the first people to arrive at the scene of the motorway pile-up?
2 Who informed the national TV companies?
3 Why does the editor read the report?
4 What happens at the 3 o'clock meeting?
5 When is the news programme planned?
6 At what time is the evening news broadcast?

Thinking about it

1 Why do you think news teams from the television companies reacted so quickly to the accident?
2 When a news team arrives, how do you think they find out what is happening?
3 What are the possible dangers to the news team at the scene of the accident?
4 Why do you think the first job the news editor does is to listen to the radio news and read the papers?
5 What do you think some of the problems are in deciding which stories to cover and which stories to leave out?

Thinking it through

1 What do you think the good and bad things are about being a television reporter?
2 What do you think this saying means: 'Yesterday's news is old news'?
3 What we see on TV is only a tiny amount of what is happening. All the news we see or hear has been chosen by someone. What are the dangers of this?
4 Some people say disaster and war take up too much space in our news. What do you think?
5 Explain what an agenda is.

UNIT 18 The Hurricane

Think ahead

Read the poem. What would it be like to be caught outdoors in a hurricane?

Shut the windows
Bolt the doors
Big rain coming
Climbing up the mountain

Neighbours whisper
Dark clouds gather
Big rain coming
Climbing up the mountain

Gather in the clothes lines
Pull down the blinds
Big wind rising
Coming up the mountain

Branches falling
Raindrops flying
Treetops swaying
People running
Big wind blowing
Hurricane! on the mountain

From *A Caribbean Dozen* by Dionne Brand

Gustus Bass, a young Jamaican boy, is sheltering from a hurricane in the schoolhouse with his family. He is worried about his banana tree at home, so he sets out to check if it is all right.

'Where's Gustus! Imogene … where's Gustus?'

'He was 'ere Pappy,' she replied, drying her eyes. I dohn know when he get up.'

Briskly, Mr Bass began combing the schoolroom to find his boy. He asked: no-one had seen Gustus. He called. There was no answer …

By this time Gustus was halfway on the mile journey to their house. The lone figure in the raging wind and shin-deep road-flood was tugging, snapping and pitching branches out of his path. His shirt was fluttering from his back like a boat-sail … As he grimaced and covered his ears he was forcefully slapped against a coconut tree trunk that laid across the road.

When his eyes opened, his round face was turned up to a festered sky. Above the tormented trees zinc sheets writhed, twisted and somersaulted in the tempestuous flurry … As Gustus turned to get up, a bullet-drop of rain struck his temple. He shook his head, held grimly to the tree trunk and struggled to his feet …

When Gustus approached the river he had to cross, it was flooded and blocked beyond recognition … The wrecked footbridge had become the harbouring fort for all the debris, branches and monstrous tree trunks which the river swept along its course. The river was still swelling. More accumulation arrived each moment, ramming and pressing the bridge. Under pressure it was cracking and shifting minutely towards a turbulent forty-foot fall.

Gustus had seen it! A feeling of dismay paralysed him, reminding him of his foolish venture … But how can he go back? He has no strength to go back. His house is nearer than the school. An' Pappy will only strap him for nothin' … for nothin' … no shoes, nothin' when the hurricane is gone...

He made a bold step and the wind half-lifted him, ducking him in the muddy flood. He sank to his neck. Floating leaves, coconut husks, dead ratbats and all manner of feathered creatures and refuse surrounded him … But he struggled on desperately until he clung to the laden bridge, and climbed up among the leafless branches …

The urgency of getting across became more frightening, and he gritted his teeth and dug his toes into the debris, climbing with maddened determination …

There was a powerful jolt. Gustus flung himself into the air and fell in the expanding water on the other side. When he surfaced, the river had dumped the entire wreckage into the gurgling gully. For once the wind helped. It blew him to land.

Gustus was in a daze when he reached his house. Mud and rotten leaves covered his head and face, and blood caked in a gash on his chin.

He could hardly recognise his yard. The terrorised trees that stood there were writhing in turmoil. Their thatched house had collapsed like an open umbrella that was given a heavy blow. He looked the other way and whispered, 'Is still dere! Dat's a miracle! Dat's a miracle!'

Dodging the wind, he staggered from tree to tree until he got to his own tormented banana tree. Gustus hugged the tree.

From *A Thief in the Village* by James Berry

 Thinking back

Write these sentences in the correct order.
As he walked the wind was raging and blowing stuff everywhere.
The bridge gave way and Gustus was thrown into the water.
Gustus was sheltering in the schoolhouse because of the hurricane.
To his surprise he found his banana tree was still standing.
The bridge was nearly cracking under the strain.
Gustus was in a daze when he reached his house.
He was worried about his banana tree so he set off home to check it.
The river was flooded.

Thinking about it

1 Who do you think Imogene is?
2 What do you think Mr Bass thought when he could not find Gustus? How do you think he felt?
3 Why do you think Gustus was worried about his banana tree? What could have been so special about it?
4 Why was it dangerous to be outside in the hurricane?
5 What sort of things would Gustus have seen and heard and felt on his journey?
6 Why did Gustus think he would get into trouble with his father?
7 What surrounded Gustus when he was blown into the muddy flood?
8 Why do you think Gustus was in a daze when he reached home?
9 What had happened to his house?
10 Why did Gustus hug the banana tree?

Thinking it through

1 Do you think Gustus was foolish or brave? Give your reasons.
2 Gustus was determined to reach his home. How can you tell this from the story?
3 How do you think Gustus felt when he reached home?
4 What do you think might happen to Gustus next?
5 The author paints a vivid picture of the hurricane. Write some of the words or phrases that he uses to show the power of the wind.
6 How can you tell the story was set in Jamaica? (There are several clues in the story.)

UNIT 19   The Tide Rises, The Tide Falls

Think ahead

What does the title of the poem make you think of?

The tide rises, the tide falls,
The twilight darkens, the curlew calls;
Along the sea-sands damp and brown
The traveller hastens to the town,
And the tide rises, the tide falls.

Darkness settles on roofs and walls;
But the sea, the sea in darkness calls;
The little waves, with their soft white hands,
Efface the footprints on the sands,
And the tide rises, the tide falls.

The morning breaks; the steeds in their stalls
Stamp and neigh, as the hostler calls;
The day returns, but nevermore
Returns the traveller to the shore,
And the tide rises, the tide falls.

From *The Tide Rises, The Tide Falls* by Henry Wadsworth Longfellow

Thinking back

Choose the best ending to complete each sentence.
1 The curlew calls a) at twilight b) at dawn
   c) in the afternoon
2 The sea-sands were a) golden brown
   b) muddy and brown c) damp and brown
3 The traveller was travelling to a) the city
   b) the town c) the village
4 Darkness settles a) on the church tower
   b) on the village green c) on roofs and walls
5 The poet says the waves have a) soft white hands
   b) watery faces c) whispering voices

 Thinking about it

1 Explain what time of day twilight is.
2 What do you think a curlew is?
3 How can you tell the traveller is in a hurry to get to town?
4 Why do you think the traveller is going to town?
5 What do you think 'the waves efface the footprints on the sand' means?
6 What other name is used for horses in the poem?
7 What do you think a 'hostler' is?

 Thinking it through

1 What time of day is each verse about? What do you notice?
2 How can you tell the poem was written some time ago?
3 Why do you think the poet keeps repeating the line 'The tide rises, the tide falls'?
4 What does the poet mean when he says that the waves have 'soft white hands'?

UNIT 20   Excalibur

Think ahead

'*Out of the lake came a shining sword, a hand holding it, and an arm in a white silk sleeve.*' What do you think Excalibur could be? What special properties could it have?

'What is this place?' I asked.

'This lake separates life from death, Arthur. Beyond the mists is the Island of Avalon. Those who live there are not living, neither are they dead. They live in a half-life. They are people not of this world, yet they can come into this world. They have earthly powers and unearthly powers, powers for good and evil. Yet the lake is just a lake like any other.'

'Where is this Excalibur?' I asked yet again. 'And what is it anyway? Can't you tell me?'

'Oh, be still with your questions, Arthur,' said Merlin. Suddenly he leaned forward and pointed. 'Look.'

I looked, but could see nothing at first. But then as I looked I saw the surface of the lake shiver and break. And, to my amazement, up out of the lake came a shining sword, a hand holding it, and an arm in a white silk sleeve.

'There,' Merlin whispered. 'You have your answer. That is Excalibur. It comes from that half-world of Avalon, the blade forged by elf-kind, the scabbard woven by the Lady Nemue herself, the Lady of the Lake, and my lady too.' And as he spoke his voice faltered. 'See, here she comes.'

And out of the mists came a figure in flowing green, walking across the water. Yet the water seemed undisturbed beneath her feet as is she was walking on air. She came towards us, holding a scabbard in both her hands, and a sword belt dangling from it. From the way she looked at Merlin and from the way he was looking at her, I could see there was an old love between them, a love still strong. There was a secret smile in her eyes and it was all for him. But when she spoke, she spoke to me.

'My Lord Arthur, I have made this for you. It is woven from

54

the gold of Avalon. Keep it always with you. Always, you hear me?'

'But the sword,' I said, 'How do I get the sword? Do I have to swim for it?'

'You will not need to,' she said, and she smiled gently. As she spoke, I saw a boat lying in amongst the reeds. Where it had come from, and how it came to be there I do not know.

'Get in,' she said.

I did not hesitate. The moment I stepped down into the boat, it moved, gliding with scarcely a sound through the dark waters out towards the arm in the middle of the lake. As we came nearer, the boat slowed and paused, only just long enough for me to reach out and take the sword by the blade. The arm withdrew into the lake. I watched until the last finger vanished.

I sat down in the bottom of the boat and examined the sword on my lap. The hilt was encrusted with jewels and gold, and fitted my grasp like no other I had ever held. The blade was broader than any I had seen before, yet it felt as light as a feather, as if it were part of my arm and not a sword at all.

The boat reached the shore and I looked up. Merlin was waiting for me, the scabbard in his hand. The Lady of the Lake was nowhere to be seen. I slid the sword into the scabbard and Merlin buckled the sword belt around my waist. He stood back to look at me. 'So, now you have Excalibur. Which do you prefer, Arthur, the sword or the scabbard?'

'The sword, of course,' I said, drawing it out for the first time. 'A scabbard without a sword is useless.'

'Not this one,' said Merlin. 'I tell you Arthur, if you do as Lady Nemue said, if you have the scabbard round your waist, then you will never loose a single drop of blood. Excalibur may bring you victory and glory and honour, it may scythe down your enemies like so much ripe corn; but the scabbard will always keep you safe. Never be parted from it, Arthur, never. She made it specially for you as a favour to me. The woman is the love of my life. One day,' he went on, musing, 'one day, I shall go to her, but not yet.' When he turned to me, his eyes were filled with tears. 'I must be with her. She is always in my head. I think you understand what I mean, don't you, Arthur?'

I understood, only too well. 'How much longer will you stay with me, Merlin?' I asked.

'A little while yet,' he said. 'A little while. And besides, I will never leave you quite alone, you know that. You will always have Bercelet.' And Bercelet came up beside me and shook himself again, showering me from head to toe.

'Oh, a comfort,' I laughed. 'A great comfort!'

And so we came home with Excalibur to Camelot.

From *Arthur, High King of Britain* by Michael Morpurgo

 Thinking back

Choose the best ending for each sentence.
1 Arthur and Merlin were standing by
   a) a river b) a lake c) the sea
2 Out of the lake came a hand holding
   a) a sword b) a dagger c) a lance
3 Out of the mists came
   a) Lady Nemur b) Lady Nemoy c) Lady Nemue
4 Merlin and Lady Nemue were
   a) old enemies b) old friends c) old lovers

5 Lying amongst the reeds was
   a) a canoe   b) a boat   c) a raft
6 The sword's hilt was encrusted with
   a) sapphires   b) rubies   c) jewels and gold
7 When Arthur reached the shore again Lady Nemue
   a) had vanished   b) said 'goodbye'   c) was sitting down
8 Merlin told Arthur that the scabbard would always
   a) shine   b) keep him safe   c) make him invisible

Thinking about it

1 What sort of people live on Avalon?
2 In what sense was the lake 'magical'?
3 Was Merlin young, middle-aged or old? How can you tell?
4 How did Arthur react when he first saw Excalibur?
5 Why do you think Merlin's voice faltered when he talked about the Lady of the Lake?
6 Why was there a 'secret smile' in Lady Nemue's eyes?
7 What do you think a scabbard is?
8 What special qualities and powers did the sword have?
9 Arthur asked Merlin how long he would stay with him. Where do you think Merlin intended to go when he left Arthur?
10 Who, or what, do you think Bercelet is? Why?

Thinking it through

1 a) Who is telling the story?   b) What is he?
  (The book title is a clue!)
2 When do you think the story takes place – in the past, in the present, in the future? Give your reasons.
3 There are many legends about King Arthur. What is a legend?
4 What do you think Camelot was? Describe how you think it might have looked.

UNIT 21   Swallows and Amazons

Think ahead

Swallows are birds. Do you think this story is going to be about birds? How can you tell without reading the whole passage?

In the holidays, John, Susan, Titty and Roger use their boat Swallow to go camping on an uninhabited island. Soon they see a strange pirate boat called Amazon and they meet the mysterious owner of the houseboat with a green parrot. Are they friends or enemies?

At that moment something hit the saucepan with a loud ping, and ashes flew up out of the fire. A long arrow with a green feather struck, quivering, among the embers. The four explorers started to their feet.

'It's begun,' said Titty.

Roger grabbed at the arrow and pulled it out of the fire.

Titty took it from him at once. It may be poisoned,' she said. 'Don't touch the point of it.'

'Listen,' said Captain John.

They listened. There was not a sound to be heard but the quiet lapping of the water against the western shore of the island.

'It's him,' said Titty. 'He's winged his arrow with a feather from his green parrot.'

'Listen,' said John again.

'Shut up, just for a minute,' said mate Susan.

There was a sharp crack of a dead stick breaking somewhere in the middle of the island.

'We must scout,' said Captain John. 'I'll take one end of the line, the mate the other. Titty and Roger go in the middle.

Spread out. As soon as one of us sees him, the others close in to help.'

They spread out across the island, and began to move forward. But they had not gone ten yards when John gave a shout.

'Swallow has gone,' he shouted. He was on the left of the line, and as soon as he came out of the camping ground he saw the landing-place where he had left Swallow when he came back with the milk. No Swallow was there. The others ran to the landing-place. There was not a sign of Swallow. She had simply disappeared.

'Spread out again. Spread out again,' said John. 'We'll comb the whole island. Keep a look-out, Mister Mate, from your shore. She can't have drifted far away. He's taken her, but he's still on the island. We heard him.'

'Roger and I pulled her right up,' said Titty. 'She couldn't have drifted off.'

'Spread out again,' said Captain John. 'Then listen. Advance as soon as the mate blows her whistle. A hoot like an owl

means all right. Three hoots means something's up. Blow as soon as you're ready, Mister Mate.'

The mate crossed the island nearly to the western shore. She looked out through the trees. Not a sail was to be seen on the lake. Far away there was the smoke of the morning steamer, but that did not count. Roger and Titty, half a dozen yards apart, were in the middle of the island. Captain John moved a little way inland, but not so far that anyone could be between him and the shore without being seen. They listened. There was not a sound.

Then, over on the western side of the island, the mate blew her whistle.

The four began moving again through the trees and undergrowth.

'Roger,' called Titty. 'Have you got a weapon?'

'No,' said Roger. 'Have you?'

'I've got two sticks, pikes, I mean. You'd better have one.'

She threw one of her sticks to Roger.

An owl hooted away to the left.

'That must be the captain,' she said. She hooted back. Susan on her right hooted in reply. And again they listened. Then they moved forward again.

'Hullo,' said Roger. 'Someone's been here.'

Titty ran to him. There was a round place where the grass and ferns were pressed flat as if someone had been lying there.

'He's left his knife,' said Roger, holding up a big clasp knife that he had found in the grass.

Titty hooted like an owl three times.

The captain and the mate came running.

'He must be quite close to,' said Titty.

'We've got his knife, anyway,' said Roger.

Captain John bent down and felt the flattened grass with his hand.

'It's not warm,' he said.

'Well, it wouldn't stay warm very long,' said the mate.

At that moment there was a wild yell …

From *Swallows and Amazons* by **Arthur Ransome**

 Thinking back

1 Who did the boat called 'Swallow' belong to?
2 What struck the saucepan?
3 Why did Titty not want Roger to touch the arrow?
4 Where did they think the green feather on the arrow had come from?

5 What noise did they hear coming from the middle of the island?
6 Who discovered 'Swallow' had gone?
7 What was the signal to advance?
8 What weapons did Roger and Titty carry?
9 How did Roger know he had found a place where someone had been?
10 What else did Roger find in the grass?

Thinking about it

1 What did Titty mean when she said, 'It's begun'?
2 Who do you think fired the arrow? Why?
3 Who is the leader of the group? How do you know?
4 Do you think the 'mysterious' owner of the 'Amazon' is an enemy or not? Why?
5 Do you think the Swallow drifted off on her own? What do you think happened? Explain your answer.
6 When they were searching the island how did they keep in touch with each other?
7 Why did John feel the flattened grass with his hand?
8 Who do you think gave the yell at the end? Why?

Thinking it through

1 What sort of story do you think this is – animal, ghost, adventure, mystery? Why?
2 How does the author try to keep you interested?
3 Do you think this could really have happened or is it unlikely? Say why.
4 What do you think the dangers could be in a group of children going off camping on an island on their own?
5 What do you think happens at the end? Continue the story.

UNIT 22 A Visitor in the Night

Think ahead

Read the introduction to the story. Look for the clues.
What do you think the passage is going to be about?

Mary's parents die in India and she is sent to live at her uncle's house in Yorkshire. Mary thinks she is the only child in the house, but one night …

Mary had been lying awake, turning from side to side for about an hour, when suddenly something made her sit up in bed and turn her head towards the door listening. She listened and listened.

'It isn't the wind now,' she said in a loud whisper. 'That isn't the wind. It is different. It is that crying I heard before.'

The door of her room was ajar and the sound came from down the corridor, a far-off sound of fretful crying. She listened for a few minutes and each minute she became more and more sure. She felt as if she must find out what it was. Perhaps the fact that she was in a rebellious mood made her bold. She put her foot out of the bed and stood on the floor.

'I am going to find out what it is,' she said. 'Everybody is in bed and I don't care about Mrs Medlock – I don't care!'

There was a candle by her bedside and she took it up and went softly out of the room. The corridor looked very long and dark, but she was too excited to mind that. She thought she remembered the corners she must turn to find the short corridor with the door covered with tapestry – the one Mrs Medlock had come through the day she lost herself. The sound had come up that passage. So she went on with her dim light, almost feeling her way, her heart beating so loud that she fancied she could hear it. The far-off, faint crying went on and led her. Sometimes it stopped for a moment or so and then it began again. Was this the right corner to turn? She stopped and thought. Yes, it was. Down this passage and then to the left, and then turn up two broad steps, and then to the right again. Yes. There was the tapestry door.

She pushed it open very gently and closed it behind her, and she stood in the corridor and could hear the crying quite plainly, though it was not loud. It was on the other side of the wall at her left and a few yards farther on there was a door. She could see a glimmer of light coming from beneath it. The Someone was crying in that room, and it was quite a young Someone.

So she walked to the door and pushed it open, and there she was, standing in the room!

It was a big room, with ancient, handsome furniture in it. There was a low fire glowing faintly on the hearth and a night-light burning by the side of a carved four-poster bed hung with brocade, and on the bed was lying a boy, crying pitifully.

Mary wondered if she was in a real place or if she had fallen asleep again and was dreaming without knowing it.

The boy had a sharp delicate face, the colour of ivory, and he seemed to have eyes too big for it. He also had a lot of hair which tumbled over his forehead in heavy locks and made his thin face seem even smaller. He looked like a boy who had been ill, but was crying more as if he were tired and cross than as if he were in real pain.

Mary stood near the door with her candle in her hand, holding her breath. Then she crept across the room, and as she drew nearer, the light attracted the boy's attention and he turned his head on his pillow and stared at her, his grey eyes opening so wide that they seemed immense.

'Who are you?' he said at last in a half-frightened whisper. 'Are you a ghost?'

From *The Secret Garden* by Frances Hodgson Burnett

Thinking back

Say if these sentences are true (T) or false (F).
1 Mary had heard the sound of crying before.
2 The sound came from the attic.
3 Mary took a lantern to light the way.
4 Mary was in a big house with lots of rooms.
5 The door of the boy's bedroom had a mirror on it.
6 In the bedroom, the boy was sitting in an armchair, crying.
7 The boy looked ill.

 Thinking about it

1 Why do you think Mary could not sleep?
2 Who do you think Mrs Medlock was?
3 Why did Mary 'almost have to feel' her way down the corridor?
4 What two clues told Mary there was someone in the room before she even opened the door?
5 Describe how the boy's bedroom was furnished.
6 Describe the boy.
7 Was the boy surprised to see Mary? How can you tell?

 Thinking it through

1 Why might Mary have felt very strange in this house?
2 The author manages to create a rather 'creepy' atmosphere. Give some examples of how she does this.
3 How can you tell Mary is excited? Find a sentence or some words from the passage that tell you.
4 How does the author make you feel sorry for the boy?
5 Think of five things you would say to persuade someone who hasn't read the passage to do so.